★ It's My State!

CONNECTICUT

The Constitution State

Michael Burgan, Stephanie Fitzgerald, Gerry Boehme

Cavendish Square

New York

Published in 2015 by Cavendish Square Publishing, LLC
243 5th Avenue, Suite 136, New York, NY 10016

Library of Congress Cataloging-in-Publication Data

Boehme, Gerry.
Connecticut / Gerry Boehme, Michael Burgan, Stephanie Fitzgerald. — Third edition.
pages cm. — (It's my state!)
Includes index.
ISBN 978-1-50260-005-9 (hardcover) ISBN 978-1-50260-006-6 (ebook)
1. Connecticut—History. I. Burgan, Michael. Connecticut. II. Title.

F94.3.B87 2015
974.6—dc23

2014020999

Editor: Fletcher Doyle
Senior Copy Editor: Wendy A. Reynolds
Art Director: Jeffrey Talbot
Designer: Doug Brooks
Senior Production Manager: Jennifer Ryder-Talbot
Production Editor: David McNamara
Photo Research by J8 Media

CONNECTICUT
CONTENTS

State Flower: Mountain Laurel

The mountain laurel is a shrub with poisonous leaves, but it also has beautiful white-and-pink flowers that bloom from May through July. Mountain laurels thrive in woodlands and can grow as high as 15 feet (4.6 meters).

State Bird: American Robin

The American robin is actually a thrush—the largest in North America. Early settlers called it a robin because it looked like robins found in Europe. A sure sign of spring in Connecticut, American robins eat worms and the berries that grow on evergreen trees.

State Tree: Charter Oak [White Oak]

The charter oak once grew in Hartford. According to legend, colonists used the charter oak to hide Connecticut's charter, a political document defining its rights as an English colony, when British authorities tried to seize it. Unfortunately, the charter oak fell during a storm in 1856.

CONNECTICUT

POPULATION: 3,574,097

★ State Insect: European Mantis

This insect, also known as the praying mantis, lives in the state from May or June until the cold weather starts. The praying mantis helps farmers by eating caterpillars and aphids as well as flies and other insects. It's called a praying mantis because it holds its two front legs close together, like hands during prayer.

★ State Fossil: *Eubrontes giganteus*

More than 200 million years ago, a meat-eating dinosaur roamed the area now known as the Connecticut River Valley. It left behind three-toed footprints called Eubrontes giganteus. About two thousand of these stony prints are located at Dinosaur State Park in Rocky Hill, but no skeletal remains have ever been found.

★ State Animal: Sperm Whale

During the 1800s, Connecticut ranked second only to Massachusetts in whale hunting. People hunted sperm whales for their blubber and other oily fluids to make products like soap, candles and lubricants. The sperm whale is now on the federal **endangered** species list.

The ocean can be enjoyed at Greenwich Point Park and many other beaches in Connecticut.

1

The Constitution State

Connecticut is a small state with a long name. The name of the state and the river comes from the Algonquian word *Quinnehtukqut*. This means "place of the long river."

Connecticut is one of the six New England states that form the northeastern corner of the United States, along with Maine, New Hampshire, Vermont, Massachusetts, and Rhode Island. Connecticut's shape is almost rectangular, with what looks like a handle sticking out of the southwestern corner. The state contains eight counties and is only 110 miles (177 kilometers) wide and 70 miles (113 km) long. With an area of approximately 5,018 square miles (12,997 sq km), Connecticut is larger than only two other states, Delaware and Rhode Island.

The surface of Connecticut was formed over millions of years. About eighteen thousand years ago, large masses of ice called glaciers covered what is now Connecticut as well as other parts of North America. As the glaciers moved, they carved out valleys. When the ice began to melt, soil and rocks were deposited across the land, helping to shape hills and other rocky features.

Today, Connecticut can be divided into four major regions: the Connecticut River Valley, the Coastal Lowlands, the Western Uplands and the Eastern Uplands. In general,

The Connecticut River provides recreation to people along the length of the state.

Connecticut Borders

North:	Massachusetts
South:	New York [Long Island Sound]
East:	Rhode Island
West:	New York

the eastern and western portions of Connecticut are very rocky and not good for farming, while the central portion of the state contains a fertile valley.

River Valley

The Connecticut River dominates the center of the state. At 410 miles (660 km) long, it is the longest river in New England. The river starts in a small beaver pond near the New Hampshire/Canada border. Moving south, it divides New Hampshire and Vermont. It then passes through Massachusetts and Connecticut. The Connecticut River's course is fairly straight in the northern half of the state before it twists and turns down to Long Island Sound. Shallow waters and **sandbars**—ridges of sand formed by waves and currents—make it hard to sail at the mouth of the river. Unlike many large U.S. rivers, the Connecticut River does not have a major port or city at its mouth. Still, the river has been an important waterway for moving goods and people.

The land on either side of the river is called the Connecticut Valley, or Central Valley. Water from the river makes the valley perfect for growing crops. Native Peoples from various tribes were the first to farm this land. The rich farmland later drew Europeans to the area.

Connecticut's capital, Hartford, sits on the western bank of the river.

Central Lowlands

The Connecticut River travels south until it empties into Long Island Sound. The land that stretches along the length of the sound forms another region of Connecticut called the Coastal Lowlands, or Coastal Slope. The land here is mostly flat, with marshlands and small coves that cut into the shoreline.

By the 1960s, pollution choked the waters of the Connecticut River and affected Long Island Sound as well. Factories and towns had been dumping waste into the river for more

The Connecticut River Valley farmland is fertile.

CONNECTICUT
COUNTY MAP

LITCHFIELD

HARTFORD

TOLLAND

WINDHAM

NEW LONDON

MIDDLESEX

NEW HAVEN

FAIRFIELD

CONNECTICUT
POPULATION BY COUNTY

Fairfield County	916,829	New London County	274,055
Hartford County	894,014	Tolland County	152,691
Litchfield County	189,927	Windham County	118,428
Middlesex County	165,676		
New Haven County	862,477		

Source: U.S. Bureau of the Census, 2010

Fall foliage is a popular attraction throughout Connecticut.

than one hundred years, killing animals and plants that live in the water. The New England states and the U.S. government have spent millions of dollars to clean up the river. Today, some sections are clean enough for swimming and fishing.

Western Uplands

Hills dot the landscape in the area west of the river called the Western Uplands. The northwest corner of the state includes Connecticut's highest point, the southern side of Mount Frissell, which reaches a height of 2,380 feet (725 m). Mount Frissell is part of a region called the Berkshire Hills. Most of this mountain, including its peak, is actually located in Massachusetts.

Bear Mountain is the tallest peak located entirely within Connecticut's borders, standing 2,323 feet (708 m) high. It is located just east of Mount Frissell. The **Appalachian Trail**, which stretches from Georgia to Maine, crosses Bear Mountain.

The Western Uplands contain one major river, the Housatonic. It begins in Massachusetts and runs through the western section before draining into Long Island Sound. The Housatonic's fast-moving waters once provided power for many mills and factories by running generators that created electricity. This kind of electricity is called **hydroelectricity**, or hydropower.

The state's two largest lakes are also in this region. Candlewood Lake

The Litchfield Hills in the Western Uplands are a great place for a fall hike.

and Barkhamsted Reservoir were not made by natural forces, but by people. Candlewood Lake, Connecticut's largest lake, was created in 1928 to provide hydroelectric power. The lake is also very popular with Connecticut residents and visitors. The lake has 60 miles (97 km) of shoreline and cuts through several towns. Many people have homes along its peaceful shores, with boaters and swimmers filling the lake in the warmer months.

The western town of Kent is home to Kent Falls, a state park that features the highest waterfall in Connecticut. It drops around 250 feet (76 m). Visitors hike and picnic along the trails.

Eastern Uplands

The region east of the Connecticut River is called the Eastern Uplands. The Eastern Uplands are not quite as high as the Western Uplands. Some spots have many hills, but in other places, flat areas of land are used for farming and raising dairy cows. The U.S. government maintains a major naval submarine base at the mouth of the Thames River in New London.

Candlewood Lake is the largest freshwater body in the state.

10 KEY SITES ★ ★ ★ ★

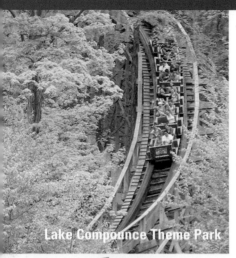

Lake Compounce Theme Park

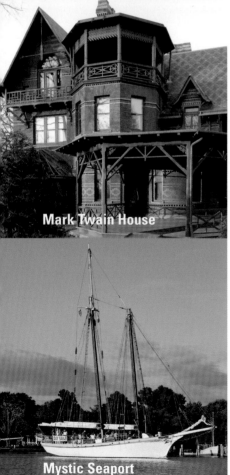

Mark Twain House

Mystic Seaport

1. Beardsley Zoo

Bridgesley's Beardsley Zoo, the only zoo in the state, is situated on 52 acres (21 hectares) in historic Beardsley Park. The zoo features three hundred animals representing nearly one hundred species.

2. Connecticut Science Center

Located in Hartford, the Connecticut Science Center features both educational and entertaining experiences and exhibits. You can dig for dinosaur bones, build a race car, or explore our solar system.

3. Lake Compounce Theme Park

Bristol's Lake Compounce is America's oldest and longest-running theme park. The park features more than fifty rides and attractions, including Boulder Dash, voted the number-one wooden roller coaster in the world.

4. Mark Twain House & Museum

Author Mark Twain built this house in Hartford and lived in it for 17 years, from 1874 to 1891. He wrote some of his most famous works here, including *The Adventures of Tom Sawyer*.

5. Mystic Seaport and Aquarium

Mystic Aquarium is the place to discover whales, penguins, sea lions and other marine animals. Mystic Seaport brings visitors back to the nineteenth century with guided tours of the waterfront's tall ships, including the *Charles W. Morgan*, the last remaining wooden **whaling** ship in the world.

6. Naugatuck Railroad

The town of Thomaston is the home of the Naugatuck Railroad and the Railroad Museum of New England. Visitors can board vintage train cars for a scenic ride along the Naugatuck River.

7. Old Lighthouse Museum

The Connecticut coast contains many lighthouses, some of which can be seen up close by taking a ferry or visiting by land. The Old Lighthouse Museum in Stonington contains many historical items, and lets visitors climb to the top of the tower.

8. Philip Johnson Glass House

American architect Philip Johnson built this rectangular house in New Canaan in 1949 out of quarter-inch-thick (6.35 millimeters) glass and without interior walls. With no curtains or blinds, the property's 47 acres (19 ha) of trees and landscaping are the only things providing privacy.

9. Putnam Memorial State Park

Putnam Memorial State Park in Redding includes the remains of Major General Israel Putnam's encampments from the winter of 1778-79. It includes log buildings and a Revolutionary War museum.

10. USS *Nautilus* and Submarine Force Museum

The Submarine Force Museum in Groton maintains the world's finest collection of submarine artifacts, and is the only submarine museum operated by the United States Navy. The USS *Nautilus*, the world's first ship to run on nuclear power, is based here. The *Nautilus* is Connecticut's State Ship and a National Historic Landmark.

Old Lighthouse Museum

Philip Johnson Glass House

The *Nautilus*

Winter brings many opportunities for recreation.

Storm Damage

Superstorm Sandy pounded the region on October 29, 2012. State officials say the storm killed five people and damaged more than thirty-eight thousand homes. It wasn't the biggest natural disaster in the state's history, however. A hurricane in 1938 created floods that destroyed buildings along Long Island Sound and Connecticut's rivers. Almost seven hundred people died across New England.

Climate and Seasons

The weather in Connecticut changes with the seasons. In summer, the air can be humid and temperatures can rise above 90 degrees Fahrenheit (32 degrees Celsius). Autumn tends to be cool and sunny, as the leaves change from green to red, yellow, and gold. In the winter, parts of the state can get more than 4 feet (1.2 m) of snow, but temperatures are usually not bitterly cold. In general, the western hills receive more snow and have colder weather than the rest of the state. Strong winds and waves from storms can strike at any time of the year, damaging houses and flooding roads along Long Island Sound. Connecticut is sometimes hit by **nor'easters**, large storms that form when northern and southern storm fronts collide. The amount of snow or rain from one nor'easter can vary quite a bit from north to south. The Western Uplands might receive as much as 1 foot(30 centimeters) of snow, while the shoreline

A couple of young white-tailed deer venture into a field seeking food.

is hit only with rain. Flooding can also occur early in the spring, when melting snow along the Connecticut River raises the water level and floods nearby land.

Wildlife of Fields, Forests, and Streams

Forests cover around 60 percent of Connecticut, and the state is home to many kinds of trees, flowers, and other plants. Oak, maple, and ash are some of the common leafy trees that grow in the state. Evergreen trees, such as pine and fir, also are common.

Many different kinds of animals live in these forests and nearby fields. One of the most common mammals is the white-tailed deer. Farmers and homeowners use wire fences or special plantings to help stop deer from eating crops as well as other plants and shrubs. Connecticut also allows deer hunting in certain seasons to prevent some animals from overpopulating.

Some animals that once lived in Connecticut left the region or died off as people cut down forests to build homes. In recent years, some of these animals, such as coyotes, have returned to the state. Families are now warned to keep their pets in at night so they will not become dinner for any prowling coyotes.

Common birds in Connecticut include robins, sparrows, and crows. The number of wild turkeys roaming through the forests—or across backyards—continues to rise. Bald eagles also live in the state, though they are few and endangered.

Many different types of fish swim in Connecticut's waters. Among them is the shad. The roe, or eggs, of this fish are considered a dinner treat. Each May, the town of Windsor has a festival honoring the shad.

The majestic peregrine falcon is slowly making a comeback in Connecticut.

Along Long Island Sound, fishers catch shellfish such as lobsters and oysters. Oysters from Connecticut are very popular. In 1997 and 1998, however, a sudden rise in the water temperature almost destroyed Connecticut's oyster fishing industry. The higher temperature encouraged the growth of small deadly organisms that target oysters. Thousands of acres of shellfish were killed. To prevent this kind of disaster from happening again, marine biologists are breeding hardier, parasite-resistant oysters. In the twenty-first century, Connecticut's oyster industry is enjoying a slow but steady recovery.

Pollution has hampered the Connecticut fishing industry.

Endangered Animals

Some animals in Connecticut are considered endangered. This means that their numbers are very small and that they are at risk of disappearing completely. When an animal or plant is listed as endangered, it becomes illegal to kill it or hurt its habitat.

The peregrine falcon is an example of an endangered bird in the state. One of the world's fastest birds, they can reach speeds of 175 miles per hour (282 kmh) when diving for food. Peregrines were once common in Connecticut and the rest of North America. However, by 1950 none of these birds were left in the state. They suffered from the use of chemical pesticides and later joined the national list of endangered animals.

The U.S. government worked to increase the number of peregrines. It raised babies and then released them in the wild. In 1997, a pair of peregrine falcons settled in Hartford. They built a nest on the Travelers Tower, one of the state's tallest buildings. The pair then had chicks. The following year, more peregrines returned to Hartford, and several others built nests in nearby cities. Although the peregrine falcon is no longer on the national list of endangered animals, the state of Connecticut still considers it threatened.

Black Bear

Bullfrog

Canada Goose

1. American Robin

American robins can often be seen tugging earthworms out of the ground. Robins are popular birds for their warm orange breast, cheery song, and early appearance at the end of winter. American robins are at home both in towns and in wilder areas.

3. Black Bass

Two kinds of black bass—smallmouth and largemouth—live in many of Connecticut's lakes and ponds. They eat other fish, insects and even birds. Each year, the state adds new bass to lakes, where anglers spend quiet days trying to catch them.

2. Black Bear

Black bears once filled Connecticut's forests, but their numbers fell as towns grew. By the mid-1800s they were mostly gone from the state. Black bears started returning after farming decreased and forests began to grow back. There were 3,358 black bear sightings in the state from May 2013 to May 2014.

4. Bullfrog

Bullfrogs are the largest type of frog in North America. They live all over Connecticut in lakes and streams. They appear in warm months after hibernating underwater for the winter. Adult bullfrogs eat creatures like mice, small birds and other frogs.

5. Canada Goose

While many types of geese migrate south for the winter, Connecticut's Canada geese stay all year long. These birds can be a nuisance in parks, ball fields, golf courses, and lawns due to their droppings!

CONNECTICUT

6. Maple Tree

Many different kinds of maple trees grow across Connecticut, including the red, silver, and sugar. In the fall, their leaves turn yellow and red, adding to the colors of the season. In March, people tap sugar maples to make maple syrup.

7. Oak Tree

Oak trees are large and require lots of water to survive, sometimes more than 50 gallons (189 liters) a day. Many animals feed on acorns that fall from oak trees.

8. Timber Rattlesnake

One of two venomous snakes in Connecticut, the timber rattlesnake lives in the rocky parts of some forests. Town governments once paid hunters for killing rattlesnakes, but now the reptile is endangered in the state and protected by law.

9. Wild Turkey

Connecticut's first settlers found wild turkeys everywhere. By the early 1800s, the bird had disappeared because of hunting and the loss of forests. In recent years, state officials brought wild turkeys back to Connecticut, and now they live in almost every town.

10. Witch Hazel

In October, this plant blooms with small yellow flowers. Witch hazel is known for the lotion made from its bark and twigs. Native Americans showed Connecticut settlers how to use the plant to treat insect bites and wounds. Today, a Connecticut company is one of the world's leading producers of witch hazel.

Timber Rattlesnake

Wild Turkey

Witch Hazel

The Saybrook Breakwater Light sits
near the site of the Saybrook Colony,
which was started in 1635.

From the Beginning

Over the years, Connecticut has experienced incredible changes in its landscape, population, and lifestyles. Farmers cut down forests to cultivate the land, only to see forests reappear as people moved from farms to towns and cities. Workers moved from agriculture to manufacturing, and after that to advanced technology, service, and entertainment media. The population grew more and more diverse as people from distant places flowed into the state, looking to improve their lives.

Through it all, Connecticut has managed to maintain a balance that provides its people with a combination of modern opportunity, natural beauty, and a sense of history that goes back centuries.

In 1614, a Dutch explorer named Adriaen Block sailed up the Connecticut River almost as far as what is now Massachusetts. He found a Native American fort along the river near the area that became Hartford. More Dutch returned to Connecticut to trade with the Native Americans, but they did not settle in the area.

First European Arrival

The English were the first Europeans to build homes and raise families along the Connecticut River. By 1630, two separate groups of English settlers had reached Massachusetts, just north of Connecticut. The Pilgrims lived in Plymouth. In Boston,

HOOKER'S EMIGRATION TO CONNECTICUT

Thomas Hooker and his followers settled in Connecticut in 1636.

people known as **Puritans** had just arrived. Both groups were Protestants. They came to North America to practice their religion because England did not give them the freedom to worship as they chose. Besides religious freedom, this new land across the Atlantic Ocean offered settlers a chance to make new and more **prosperous** lives.

In 1631, Native Americans from the Podunk tribe located in the Connecticut region traveled to Plymouth. They invited the Pilgrims to come live and trade on their land. The Podunks also wanted English military aid to stop raids carried out by the Pequot tribe. In 1633, a small group of English traders built a trading post in what is now Windsor.

That same year, some Puritans explored the Connecticut Valley. One of them said the area had "many very desirable places . . . fit to receive many hundred inhabitants." Soon more English came to trade and farm along the Connecticut River. The largest group, Puritans led by Thomas Hooker, reached Hartford in 1636. Other Puritans went to today's Saybrook, at the mouth of the Connecticut River, and to New Haven, on Long Island Sound.

Although some Native Americans welcomed the English, others did not. The Europeans brought goods and trade items that proved useful, but they also brought diseases to which Native Americans had no resistance. As a result, many of the Native inhabitants died of illnesses such as smallpox.

Many English settlers also did not respect the Native Americans' ways of life and their rights to the land. Some English settlers felt that they had a claim to the land even though the Native Americans had been living there for many years. They did not understand the religions of the Native Americans and considered them uncivilized people who did not believe in Christianity. While some Natives were persuaded to become Christians and adopt the ways of the Europeans, others resisted the English people's growing power.

The English settlers' relations with the Pequots were especially poor. The Pequots did not want to lose lands to the new arrivals. They stood against the English and the Native tribes who sided with them. In 1637, small conflicts between the Pequots and the English turned into the Pequot War. The English troops had the support of another tribe, the Mohegans, and their chief, Uncas. Together, they attacked and burned many Pequot villages.

Some historians believe that this defeat of the Pequots was a turning point for English colonization. The English gained new allies and no longer had to face this large and powerful group of Native Americans opposed to their settlements.

Ivy League

Yale University, founded in 1701 in New Haven, is one of eight Ivy League schools, along with Brown, Columbia, Cornell, Dartmouth, Harvard, Pennsylvania, and Princeton. Seven of the Ivy League schools were founded before the American Revolution: Cornell was founded just after the American Civil War. People believe that the term "ivy league" was first used by a sportswriter describing the ivy-covered walls of these long established colleges.

War with the colonists devastated the Pequot.

The Native People

The Native Americans first arrived in the region about ten thousand years ago. Historian Brent Colley of Redding has rediscovered early paths throughout the state that later became Route 1 and other Connecticut roads. As many as ten thousand Native Americans may have lived in the area that became Connecticut when Europeans first arrived. The northeast section of Connecticut and part of Massachusetts was occupied by the Nipmuck tribe. Southeastern Connecticut was occupied by the Mohegan and Pequot tribes, which are often thought of as one group. The northwest part of the state was occupied by the Mahican, who also controlled much of New York. In the Southwest were the Quiripi (including Mattabesic, Paugusett, and Schaghticoke). There were other tribes, including the Podunk. Just before the Europeans arrived, the Pequots conquered more than half of the state. These tribes spoke a language called Algonquian.

The Native People's diet was a varied one. They raised beans, squash, and corn. They also hunted, fished, and collected nuts and berries. They made their homes from trees and brush that grew in the woods. All parts of the hunted animals were used for things such as food and clothing. Many of their implements (axes, gouges, arrowheads, and knives) were made of stone. Wood was commonly used to make utensils, bowls, and pipes with beautiful carvings on them. Containers were made from tree bark.

This statue of a Mohegan family is next to the Mohegan Tribal Memorial.

The most common shelter built by Native Americans was a wigwam, which was generally dome-shaped. The men would collect saplings and place them upright in a circle on the ground. The saplings were bent and tied together, then covered with bark or woven mats depending on the weather. A hole was cut in the top to allow smoke of the campfire to escape. The entrance was made from the skin of an animal hung over an opening.

Epidemics and warfare nearly wiped out the Native American tribes in Connecticut, so they had to merge to survive. All of their languages were lost. Many were driven from their lands, although some, such as the Pequot, were allowed to return to reservations close to their original homes.

Today there are two federally recognized tribes in Connecticut: the Mashantucket Pequot Tribe and the Mohegan Tribe. In addition, the state recognizes two additional tribes: the Eastern Pequot Tribal Nation and the Schaghticokes Tribal Nation.

Spotlight on the Mohegan

In the early 1660s, the Mohegan tribe split with the Pequots after disagreeing about how to handle the European settlers. The Mohegans favored collaboration with the English and joined them to fight the Pequots. The Mohegans helped the English defeat the Pequots, which helped keep Mohegans relatively safe during later wars.

Clothing: Clothing was fashioned from fur and leather as well as from twined materials, often insulated with feathers. Twining is a weaving technique wrapping and twisting two weft strands around a warp strand.

Art: Mohegans were known for making mats and baskets. Dolls made of household items were used to remind children that nothing should be wasted.

Roles: Female Mohegan members traditionally worked in the fields, prepared food, and cared for children, while men hunted and protected the tribe. However, women often held positions of great responsibility. Women traditionally chose tribal leaders.

Today: For over 350 years, treaties and laws have highlighted the tribe's independent status. The U.S. federal government formally recognized the Mohegan Nation on March 7, 1994. Today, the Mohegan Nation controls its own government and lands. After the passage of the Native American Indian Gaming Regulatory Act (IGRA) in 1988, the Mohegans successfully built the Mohegan Sun Casino, which shares hundreds of millions of dollars of revenue with Connecticut. Connecticut's Native American tribes are now the single largest source of revenue for Connecticut outside of the federal government.

Cooper Caused Confusion

People sometimes think Mohegans and Mahicans [sometimes spelled Mohicans] were the same people, but they were different tribes. The Mohegans named their tribe after their word for "wolf," while the Mahicans named themselves after the Hudson River. The confusion may have started when English settlers had trouble pronouncing their Native American names. Author James Fenimore Cooper contributed to the confusion in his classic book *Last of the Mohicans* when he gave some Mohican characters Mohegan names and placed their homeland in Mohegan territory.

Forming a Government

In 1639, the Hartford settlement drafted rules for forming its own government. Thomas Hooker told the settlers, "The foundation of authority is . . . in the free consent of the people." The settlers would elect people to represent their common interests, much as in Massachusetts. However, the Connecticut settlers were the first Americans to write down the rules for their government, called the Fundamental Orders. The rules for forming a government can also be called a constitution. Because of the importance of the Fundamental Orders, Connecticut is known as the Constitution State.

Although the English settlers in Connecticut now had their own government, they were still tied to England, their home country. In 1662,

This painting depicts the signing of the Fundamental Orders in 1639.

Connecticut received a charter from England. This legal document made the different settlements in Connecticut part of one colony. The charter also allowed the residents to keep the government they had already formed.

Most English settlers in Connecticut were farmers. They belonged to the Congregational Church, which was the church of the Puritans. Even though the Puritans left England in part for religious freedom, the settlers decided that only members of this church could freely practice their religion in the colony. This limit on religious freedom kept other Europeans from coming to Connecticut.

After another war between colonists and native tribes in 1676 known as King Philip's War, Connecticut became mostly peaceful for the English settlers. However, the Native Americans were almost wiped out. Many died from illnesses the English

The Law Library of the University of Connecticut Law School is one of the largest in the world.

Making Antique Documents

Some important Connecticut documents date back many years. You can create copies that look like original antiques. You can also use this antique paper process on things like invitations and letters. Follow these steps to age your brand-new paper instantly for a neat, old-fashioned look.

What You Need

Paper

A wet, used tea bag

Damp coffee grounds

Lemon juice

A flame

An iron

What To Do

- Write something on the paper. Then drag a wet tea bag across it. The tea will stain the paper, giving it an aged appearance.

- Place damp coffee grounds on the paper; then shake them off. The coffee will turn the paper brown and give it an aged appearance.

- Cover the paper with lemon juice. Then, with the help of an adult, carefully expose it near a flame. Be careful—don't burn it! The longer the exposure, the darker the paper will become. Tea, coffee, and lemon juice are all acidic, and will decrease the life of the paper.

- Tear the edges a little bit, then wet the inner borders slightly to keep from burning more of the paper than you want. Then, carefully burn the paper's edges.

- Carefully crumple the paper a couple of times, and then iron it.

- Now, show everyone your antique document.

brought with them. Others had died in the wars, or had left the region when they lost their lands.

The colony grew even more during the 1700s. Farmers raised crops such as corn, rye, and barley. Some residents worked building ships, while others made iron or ground wheat into flour at mills set up along rivers. Many Connecticut men and women ran shops, taverns, and inns. In New Haven, students attended one of the colony's first educational institutions, Yale College, now known as Yale University.

The Fight for Independence

By the mid-1770s, many Americans were calling for independence from England, now a part of Great Britain. In Connecticut, many people supported the call for freedom, but others wanted to remain part of Great Britain.

When the American Revolution began in 1775, Connecticut played an important role. Its early military heroes included General Israel Putnam. At the Battle of Bunker Hill in Boston, Putnam is said to have given the famous order, "Don't fire until you see the whites of their eyes."

Another Connecticut hero was Nathan Hale, a schoolteacher turned soldier. He

Nathan Hale's last words were recorded by a British officer present at his execution.

Connecticut's Greatest Leader

Jonathan Trumbull was the last colonial governor of Connecticut and the first governor of the state. During the American Revolution, Trumbull was the only colonial governor to side with the colonists. He was therefore the only one to remain in office throughout the war—and to be elected once the colonies gained freedom. Many historians consider Trumbull one of the state's greatest leaders.

served as an American spy during the war until the British caught and hanged him. Before he died, Hale said, "I only regret that I have but one life to lose for my country."

The American Revolution ended in 1783. Connecticut had helped win the revolution in many important ways, including supplying guns, cannons, and other supplies for the troops. These supplies were also called provisions, and George Washington nicknamed Connecticut the Provisions State. In 1788, five years after the war ended,

The *Charles W. Morgan* was used for whaling in the nineteenth century.

Connecticut became the fifth state to ratify the new U.S. Constitution.

Manufacturing and Trade

By the nineteenth century, Connecticut had little farmland left for new settlers. It was also hard for farmers already there to make a living. Its rocky landscape and small size meant that Connecticut had less fertile land than other states, making it difficult to compete in farming.

Eli Whitney's inventions helped make Connecticut a center for manufacturing.

Over time, manufacturing and trade replaced farming as the center of economic activity. Cities gained fame for making different products. Waterbury became known as the "Brass City," and Meriden became the "Silver City." Plymouth made clocks. Danbury made headwear and became "Hat City." Banks and insurance companies grew in Hartford, the "Insurance Capital." Shipbuilding remained important along the Connecticut River and Long Island Sound. New London became the center of Connecticut's whaling trade.

One newspaper writer in the mid-1800s was impressed with the number of talented people who came from the state. "Everybody worth knowing was born in Connecticut— or should have been," the journalist wrote. "It is the most extraordinary patch of land in the known world."

Traders from Connecticut traveled all over the country selling goods made in the state. These people were often called Yankee **peddlers**. The peddlers sold many items, including **nutmeg**, a spice from the seed produced by a nutmeg tree. Nutmeg is often used in pies, puddings, cakes, and cookies. Due to its popularity, Connecticut is often nicknamed the Nutmeg State, and its people are called Nutmeggers.

Bridgeport's Barnum Museum

Cove Island Park

Waterbury

1. Bridgeport: population 144,229

Bridgeport sits on Long Island Sound and is home to 13 officially delineated neighborhoods. Attractions include shoreline parks, museums, regional baseball and hockey, festivals, and national musical performances.

2. New Haven: population 129,778

Also located on the northern shore of Long Island Sound, New Haven is the home of Yale University. The city served as co-capital of Connecticut from 1701 until 1873, when Hartford was chosen as the centralized state capital.

3. Hartford: population 124,775

Hartford is Connecticut's capital and is the birthplace of the Boys & Girls Club. Hartford has been nicknamed the "Insurance Capital of the World." It was founded in 1637, and ranks among the oldest cities in the United States.

4. Stamford: population 122,643

In recent years, Stamford has grown impressively. Stamford businesses include leaders in finance, pharmaceuticals, insurance, hospitality, media, and consumer products. The Stamford Transportation Center includes the busiest train station between New York City and Boston.

5. Waterbury: population 110,366

Once the leading center in the United States for the manufacture of brassware, Waterbury was nicknamed "The Brass City." In 1932, the Waterbury Clock Company, now known as Timex, partnered with Disney on Mickey Mouse watches and clocks. Its huge success saved the company from bankruptcy.

6. Norwalk: population 85,603

Norwalk is located along the Connecticut coast between Bridgeport and Stamford. Known for its oysters, Norwalk hosts an annual Oyster Festival just after Labor Day.

7. Danbury: population 80,093

Danbury is in Fairfield County in southwest Connecticut and is close to Candlewood Lake, the largest lake in the state. Its location allows easy access to big-city activities as well as small-town New England traditions.

8. New Britain: population 73,206

Only nine miles (14 km) away from Hartford, New Britain is known for manufacturing hardware and tools. The city has the largest Polish population in the state and features the oldest museum in the United States for American art.

9. West Hartford: population 63,268

An upscale suburb of Hartford, the town of West Hartford has received many awards for its great resources and attractions. These include being named in 2010 as one of the "10 Great Cities for Raising Families" and "10 Best Cities for the Next Decade" according to *Kiplinger's Personal Finance* magazine, and the "55th best small city in America" by CNN Money.

10. Bristol: population 61,353

Located 20 miles (32 km) southwest of Hartford, Bristol is well known as the home of ESPN and to Lake Compounce, America's oldest operating theme park.

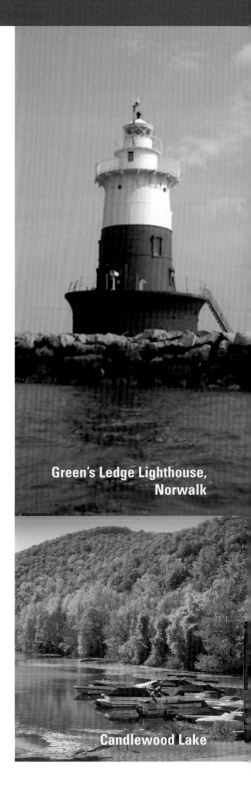

Green's Ledge Lighthouse, Norwalk

Candlewood Lake

Inventions Spur Growth

Connecticut inventors played a large role in building the state's economy. In 1836, Hartford-born Samuel Colt patented a new kind of pistol. The Colt revolver was the first firearm that could shoot five or six bullets without reloading. Before Colt's invention, only one- or two-barrel flintlock pistols were available. Colt later built a huge factory in Hartford.

Connecticut also became a leader in producing machines and tools that made other items. In 1793, a Yale graduate named Eli Whitney invented the cotton gin (short for "engine"), a machine that separates cotton fibers from seeds. Whitney then developed the idea of mass production—a faster, less expensive way to manufacture goods. Before this innovation, products such as guns were made one at a time, by hand. It took a lot of time to make each gun, and it was difficult to find replacement parts. Whitney came up with a plan to build milling machines that could easily make many identical copies of each gun part. Workers would then assemble the parts quickly and cheaply, making many guns that were exactly the same.

Whitney opened a factory in New Haven, and his ideas for mass production spread to other factories throughout the state. Through the nineteenth century, some notable products made in Connecticut included typewriters, bicycles, sewing machines, and textiles for clothing.

More Workers Needed

The new factories that appeared in Connecticut before and after the Civil War needed workers. **Immigrants** from Europe began to move to Connecticut in large numbers. The first major wave came from Ireland and Germany in the 1840s. In the decades that followed, many people arrived from southern and eastern Europe, including immigrants from Poland and Italy. Most newcomers settled in cities to work in factories, but some also bought farms.

Changing Times

While Connecticut was changing, so was the nation. Tensions stemming from differences between the Northern states and Southern states were rising. The North and the South had different economies. The Southern states depended on slavery to keep their agricultural economy going. The Northern states had more industry and did not have the same need for slaves. Some Northerners also believed that human slavery was wrong in a free society. These conflicts would lead to the outbreak of the Civil War in 1861.

Like most Northern states, Connecticut itself had a mixed past when it came to the issue of slavery. Not many slaves lived in the colony in the early 1700s. However, by the start of the American Revolution, Connecticut had the largest number of slaves in New England, although its total number of slaves (about 6,500) was much smaller than in the Southern states. Runaway slaves in Connecticut were always prosecuted and returned to their masters. The Connecticut **legislature** rejected bills to free slaves three times—in

Boys sold newspapers on the streets of Hartford in 1909. The Hartford Courant began publishing in 1764.

1777, 1779, and 1780. Even free blacks in Connecticut suffered from discrimination.

During these years there were groups in the state that worked tirelessly to end slavery. While some Northern states abolished the practice altogether, others including Connecticut enacted laws to gradually free individuals held in slavery. Connecticut passed a gradual emancipation act in 1784. Slavery was finally abolished in the state in 1848.

Even while slavery was still legal in Connecticut, some people worked to help escaped slaves find freedom. From the 1830s until the end of the Civil War, the Underground Railroad helped slaves from the South reach freedom in slave-free states. The Underground Railroad was a network that consisted of white abolitionists (people who believed slavery was wrong and fought against it), free blacks, and escaped slaves. Conductors—the people who would lead the escaped slaves north to freedom—met the slaves at a designated point in the South and led them north at night. Others gave the conductors and slaves shelter and food. Researchers have identified many buildings in Connecticut as stops along the Underground Railroad. These sites are honored as part of

The slave revolt that resulted in the death of Captain Ferrer aboard the *Amistad* in July of 1839.

the Connecticut Freedom Trail.

The story of the *Amistad* also shows how Connecticut played a part in the fight against slavery. In 1839, a group of African slaves revolted against their captors on the slave transport ship *Amistad*. The vessel eventually arrived in New London. The Africans spent more than a year in jail in New Haven, hoping to win their freedom in court. With the legal help of former U.S. president John Quincy Adams, the Africans eventually won their freedom and were allowed to go back to their homelands. Before leaving the United States, they spent almost

Switching Sides

Benedict Arnold was a respected general at the start of the Revolutionary War, when he led American troops in several major battles. The Norwich native is known today as the man who tried to surrender the American fort at West Point, New York, to the British. His name is synonymous with traitor.

a year in Farmington, where the local residents housed, clothed, and educated them. People of Connecticut also helped raise money for the Africans' journey back home. The incident has been called the most important battle for civil rights in Connecticut and may have helped the state to finally abolish slavery in 1848.

The Civil War was fought from 1861 to 1865. Connecticut sent more than fifty-thousand men to fight for the Union (the Northern states trying to preserve the United States) against the Confederacy (the eleven Southern states that had seceded from, or left, the United States). Soldiers from Connecticut included an African-American military unit called the Connecticut Twenty-Ninth Colored Regiment. Connecticut also supported the war effort by providing weapons, clothing, and food to the Union soldiers.

After the Civil War

Life in Connecticut changed after the South was defeated and the Civil War ended. By 1910, most Nutmeggers lived in cities and towns instead of on farms. Farmland was better and more plentiful in the Midwest and West, so industry became the major source of jobs in Connecticut. More and more Nutmeggers started to work in factories.

Violent abolitionist John Brown was born in Torrington.

During World War I, which lasted from 1914 to 1918, the state produced guns and other weapons. After the United States entered the war in 1917, Connecticut once again provided the nation with brave men and women who served in or worked for the military.

World War II (1939-1945) brought even more changes. Supplying engines and other parts for airplanes became the state's major industry even before the United States entered

Women kept factories like Groton's Electric Boat Company going when the state's men went off to fight in World War II.

the fight in 1941. Across Connecticut, women went to work in the factories to provide supplies and equipment during the war while their men fought overseas.

Connecticut's African-American population also continued to grow. People of color had lived in Connecticut since colonial times, both as free men/women and as slaves. During World War II, Northern factories needed workers, so many African Americans from the South headed to Connecticut for jobs, increasing the African American population even further.

Into the Modern Era

Many manufacturing companies and other businesses have moved out of the state since World War II. Companies in the service industry grew to take their place. Banks, government agencies, and schools all expanded. Companies that provided services to tourists also grew.

New businesses continue to create jobs in Connecticut. Insurance companies have expanded, and the state has become a major center for scientific and medical research. The Stamford area in particular has seen an increase in companies involved with entertainment and media. Cable sports network ESPN's headquarters and main facilities are located in Bristol, Connecticut, where the company employs more than four thousand people.

Connecticut also continues to attract people from other countries. Along with their cultures, many of these immigrants bring new ideas to the state. This creativity helps Connecticut continue to grow and move into the future.

Enrollment at the University of Connecticut and the state's other campuses has increased greatly since 1997.

10 KEY DATES IN STATE HISTORY

1. 1614

Dutch explorer Adriaen Block becomes the first European to sail up the Connecticut River and establish trade with the Native Americans in the area.

2. September 21, 1638

The Treaty of Hartford marks the end of the Pequot War as English settlers defeat the Pequots and take control of the area.

3. January 9, 1788

Connecticut becomes the fifth state to ratify the U.S. Constitution. It was drafted the previous summer in Philadelphia, where Connecticut's delegates proposed a system of government that led to the two-house legislative system still in place today.

4. 1848

Slavery is abolished in Connecticut.

5. September 21, 1938

A hurricane, which kills almost seven hundred people, becomes the state's worst natural disaster.

6. January 21, 1954

The USS *Nautilus*, the world's first nuclear-powered submarine, launches from Groton.

7. November 1974

Ella Grasso becomes the first woman to be elected as Governor of Connecticut. She was inaugurated in January 1975. She was elected to a second term in 1978, but resigned on New Year's Eve 1980 due to illness.

8. August 8, 2000

Democratic Presidential candidate Al Gore chooses Democratic Senator Joe Lieberman of Stamford to become the first Jewish vice presidential candidate from a major party. The Gore/Lieberman team won the popular vote in the Presidential election but lost a very close and controversial vote in the Electoral College to Republicans George W. Bush and Dick Cheney.

9. April 5 and April 6, 2004

"March Madness"—The University of Connecticut men's and women's basketball teams both win NCAA championships, making UConn the first school to win both Division I titles in the same year. Both teams repeat this feat in 2014.

10. December 14, 2012

Twenty-six people—twenty students and six adults—were shot and killed at the Sandy Hook Elementary School in Newtown, Connecticut, by Adam Lanza, 20, who first shot and killed his mother in their home.

Flowers decorate fields and gardens throughout Connecticut.

The People

The original inhabitants of today's Connecticut were Native Americans. They lived there for thousands of years before Europeans ventured across the ocean. From the late 1600s until the 1820s, most people who lived in Connecticut came from England or other parts of Great Britain. Almost all of them were Protestants.

Since the 1800s, Connecticut has become more diverse in its **ethnicity**, with citizens migrating from many different countries. Hispanic, African American, and Asian American populations have risen in recent years, while the number of non-Hispanic white people has fallen. Hispanics now make up more than 13 percent of the state's residents. Many are Puerto Rican, but others hail from elsewhere in Latin America. African Americans comprise approximately 11 percent of the state population, while Asians make up nearly 4 percent.

Every ten years, the U.S. government counts the number of people living in the United States. This count is called the census. According to the latest 2010 Census, Connecticut is home to more than 3.5 million people.

Religions

The people of Connecticut practice many different religions. The largest group is Roman Catholic. Many others belong to various Protestant churches, including Congregational, Episcopal, Lutheran, Methodist, and Baptist.

Who Connecticut Residents Are

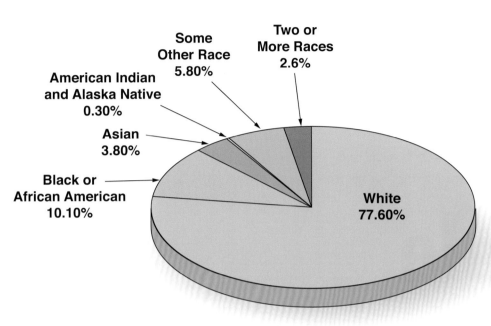

Total Population
3,574,097

American Indian
and Alaska Native
0.30%

Some
Other Race
5.80%

Two or
More Races
2.6%

Asian
3.80%

Black or
African American
10.10%

White
77.60%

Hispanic or Latino (of any race):

• **479,087 people (13.40%)**
Note: The pie chart shows the racial breakdown of the state's population based on the categories used by the U.S. Bureau of the Census. The Census Bureau reports information for Hispanics or Latinos separately, since they may be of any race. Percentages in the pie chart may not add to 100 because of rounding.

Source: U.S. Bureau of the Census, 2010 Census

Jewish settlers first came to Connecticut in the 1700s. Recently, Russian Jewish immigrants have come to the state. Newer immigrants from Eastern Europe and Asia practice religions such as Islam, Buddhism, and Hinduism. The people from these different cultures and religions have helped to shape Connecticut into the culturally diverse state it is today.

Return of the First Peoples

In 1980, only about four thousand residents in Connecticut considered themselves Native Americans. This grew to about thirty-one thousand people in the 2010 Census. Most of this growth came after the Mashantucket Pequot and the Mohegan tribal nations received federal recognition from the U.S. government. This recognition means that the tribes can run their lands as separate nations.

Many members of these tribes had left Connecticut in the past but have since returned. They can now share their heritage while living on their tribal lands. Denise Porter, a Pequot who returned, said, "I felt that [the tribal nation] was part of me. I thought, 'This is good, because I'm back home and I'm working for my own people.'"

With federal recognition, they can also run businesses of their choice. The Pequots and Mohegans have used their tribal land to build casinos, earning hundreds of millions of dollars for themselves and the state. Some of their money goes toward maintaining their lands and businesses and funding education for their young people.

The Native Americans also want to share their history and culture with others. The Mashantucket Pequots have established the Mashantucket Pequot Museum and Research Center. It includes full-size exhibits of Pequot farmers and hunters, and shows details of life from the past and present.

Some Native American groups stayed in Connecticut even after they lost their traditional lands. The Schaghticoke Reservation can be found on the New York–Connecticut border in Litchfield County. The Paucatuck Eastern Pequot Reservation is in New Windsor. These groups are proud of their heritage and often travel to schools and events across Connecticut to teach others. Many of these tribes, including the Schaghticokes and the Eastern Pequots, are still seeking recognition for their tribes from the U.S. government.

Recent immigration has added to Connecticut's diversity.

★ 10 ★ KEY PEOPLE ★ ★

P.T. Barnum

Prudence Crandall

Annie Leibovitz

1. Geno Auriemma

As head coach of the University of Connecticut's women's basketball team, Auriemma has led the Huskies to nine national titles, fifteen Final Fours, and fiveperfect seasons—all since he arrived in 1985. His record includes a record ninety-game winning streak and a strong player graduation rate.

2. P.T. Barnum

Phineas Taylor (P.T.) Barnum was born in 1810 in Bethel. Barnum will always be connected with the great American circus. He was 60 years old when he started "P.T. Barnum's Grand Traveling Museum, Menagerie, Caravan, and Circus," which he later called, "The Greatest Show on Earth."

3. Jim Calhoun

The Massachusetts-born Calhoun arrived in 1986 and turned the poorly performing UConn men's basketball team into one of the nation's best, winning three NCAA championships before retiring in 2012.

4. Prudence Crandall

Prudence Crandall faced fierce opposition when she admitted an African American student into a school for girls she founded in Canterbury, Connecticut, in 1831. She then opened a school for black children but was forced to close it after withstanding violent protests and serving a stint in jail. Crandall is the official state heroine of Connecticut.

5. Annie Leibovitz

One of America's best portrait photographers, Annie Leibovitz was born in 1949 in Waterbury. She is known for combining bold colors and surprising, sometimes controversial, poses.

CONNECTICUT

John Mayer

Seth MacFarlane

Mark Twain

6. Joseph Lieberman

Joseph Lieberman was born in 1942 in Stamford. After serving in the state senate and as Connecticut's Attorney General, Lieberman was elected to the U.S. Senate in 1988. He served until he decided not to run in 2012. In 2000, Lieberman was the first Jewish vice presidential candidate from a major party.

7. John Mayer

John Mayer was born in Bridgeport in 1977. Mayer has released six albums with musical styles ranging from acoustic rock to blues, selling more than twenty million albums worldwide. Known for many songs including "Gravity" and "Waiting On The World to Change," Mayer has won seven Grammy Awards.

8. Seth MacFarlane

The native of Kent created hit television series such as *Family Guy, American Dad!*, and *The Cleveland Show*, as well as the movie *Ted*. He also acts and supplies the voices for many of his characters, and he hosted the Academy Awards in 2013.

9. Harriet Beecher Stowe

The author was born in Litchfield in 1811 and wrote more than thirty books before her death in 1896, including *Uncle Tom's Cabin*. The best-selling book, has never been out of print.

10. Mark Twain

Born in Missouri in 1835, Mark Twain's real name was Samuel Clemens. He was already a well-known author when he settled in Hartford in 1871 and built a huge home that the local newspaper called "one of the oddest-looking buildings in the state ever designed for a dwelling."

People on the Move

Most Connecticut residents live in cities or suburbs. The state's largest cities are Bridgeport, New Haven, Hartford, and Stamford. Except for Stamford, all of these cities lost population during the 1990s. Some residents moved to find better or different jobs, or to raise their families in the quieter suburbs.

Hartford had the largest drop in population, as more than eighteen thousand people moved out. In 2001, in an effort to bring new life to the capital city, Hartford broke ground on a building project called Adriaen's Landing. Today, the site includes a convention center, a four-star hotel and a state-of-the-art science center.

Rich State, Poor State

As Connecticut's population changes, the state faces a growing problem. Many people have good jobs and live well, particularly in some of the suburbs. For example, the median family income is well over $200,000 in New Canaan and Darien in Fairfield

People can learn about Native American culture at the Mashantucket Pequot Tribal Nation powwow in North Stonington.

County. This area near Long Island Sound is sometimes called the Gold Coast, and includes some of the wealthiest areas in the United States.

Areas like these sometime lead people to assume that everyone in Connecticut is wealthy, but not all the towns and cities are as prosperous. In truth, Connecticut has a large gap between its rich and poor. Many people have trouble finding good jobs. For example, Hartford's income has fallen recently and more than 30 percent of its people now live below the poverty line. Families in other cities and towns have also seen their income drop.

This gulf between rich and poor is obvious in some of Connecticut's schools. The state boasts several of the nation's top private schools, while many of its cities and towns

Connecticut continues to build toward a better future.

also have highly regarded public schools. Connecticut also contains many highly ranked colleges and universities, including famous private institutions as well as a well-respected state university system, which includes the University of Connecticut.

However, some of Connecticut's public schools sit at the other end of the spectrum. This difference was brought to the public's attention in 1996 when Milo Sheff, a student at a Hartford middle school, sued the state. He claimed he was being denied equal education, arguing that minority children in cities like Hartford did not get the same quality of education as schoolchildren in some suburbs and smaller towns. Sheff and the others wanted the state to provide equal education for all students, regardless of where they lived. The case, known as *Sheff v. O'Neill*, went all the way to Connecticut's Supreme Court. The court ruled that the state had an obligation to make sure that all Connecticut children have access to equal levels and standards of education.

Connecticut makes providing an equal education to all students a high priority, including these at New Haven middle school.

Since the 1996 decision, Sheff plaintiffs have been working with Hartford Public Schools, the City of Hartford and the State of Connecticut to create programs that try to eliminate racial isolation in schools. These efforts have resulted in substantial gains.

More than 1,600 Hartford students now take part in Open Choice, a program that allows urban students to attend public schools in nearby suburban towns, or suburban and rural students to attend public schools in a nearby urban center. Students can also attend regional magnet schools, where they come together to learn in educational settings that offer a range of themes or teaching philosophies.

School Guarantee

Attorney Simon Bernstein of Hartford was a delegate at the 1965 Connecticut Constitutional Convention when he realized that only Connecticut did not guarantee its residents a right to an education. He drafted an amendment to the constitution and fought for it until it passed. Now, every child is guaranteed a free public education.

The Best of Connecticut

Connecticut offers many reasons for people to live in the state. Some residents like the state's location. It is close to two major cities, New York and Boston, but it also has plenty of woodlands and open spaces. For people who enjoy boating, rivers and lakes abound and Long Island Sound is nearby. Some of New England's best mountains for skiing are also close to Connecticut.

Connecticut's largest businesses provide good jobs. Connecticut has highly educated workers skilled in such areas as computers, engineering, and insurance. The state's hospitals do important medical research. Overall, many of Connecticut's schools are among the best in the nation.

Its cities offer plenty of art and entertainment. Hartford's Wadsworth Atheneum, one of the oldest public art museums in the United States, owns more than forty-five thousand pieces of art from around the world. Bridgeport is home to the state's only zoo, the Beardsley. Its New World Tropics Building features animals from the rain forests of South America.

In New Haven, Yale University's Peabody Museum displays some of the first dinosaur bones found in North America. Each June, the city sponsors the Festival of Arts and Ideas. Performers entertain on city streets and in theaters across New Haven. The state also has amusement parks, shopping malls, and other places that are perfect for relaxing and having fun. Connecticut has a lot to offer residents and visitors.

Apple Fest

Hartford Festival of Jazz

★ 1. Apple Fest in Glastonbury

October is harvest time, and this festival pays tribute to Connecticut's farming roots. The festival features a pie bake-off and a pie eating contest, as well as rides, crafts, food, and entertainment.

★ 2. Barnum Festival in Bridgeport

Every summer, Bridgeport honors its most famous resident, circus owner P. T. Barnum. The festival, which was founded in 1948, has circus performances, music, a "Got Talent" vocal competition, parades, and fireworks.

★ 3. Connecticut Flower & Garden Show in Hartford

Considered one of the most prestigious flower and garden shows in New England, the Connecticut Flower & Garden Show is held in February and features breathtaking gardens constructed by some of the Constitution State's most prolific landscape designers.

★ 4. Dogwood Festival in Fairfield, Connecticut

Held in May and a popular event for almost 80 years, the annual Dogwood Festival attracts thousands of visitors. It celebrates the beauty of springtime in Fairfield and offers many different events featuring arts and crafts.

★ 5. Hartford Festival of Jazz

For one weekend in July, Hartford's Bushnell Park is filled with the sound of music, as top jazz artists perform free concerts. The largest free jazz event in New England, which started in 1992, drew more than seventy thousand listeners in 2014.

CONNECTICUT

6. Italian Festival in Enfield

Many Connecticut towns host festivals celebrating the state's Italian immigrants. The Enfield festival, usually held in August, is one of the oldest. The fun includes games, music, rides, and of course, plenty of Italian food.

7. Open Cockpit Sundays in Windsor Locks

On several Sundays throughout the year, the New England Air Museum lets visitors explore the cockpits of some of the aircraft in its collection. The museum also features a Flight Sim Spot, where you can be in control of a plane, and Build and Fly activities.

8. Oyster Festival in Norwalk

Each year in September, Norwalk celebrates its most famous shellfish with food, music, games and rides, environmental demonstrations, and harbor cruises.

9. Sea Music Festival in Mystic

The three-day Sea Music Festival is held in June and attracts more than five thousand enthusiasts from all over the world. It features concerts, workshops, and the Music of the Sea Symposium, a two-day program exploring the links between sea, music, and song.

10. Shakespeare on the Sound

Every summer, this theater troupe produces free outdoor festivals in Connecticut, with performances in Rowayton and Greenwich. There is an education tent in which children can watch a pre-show and do arts and crafts, puzzles, and word searches.

New England Air Museum

Oyster Festival

Mystic Harbor

The Connecticut State Capitol became
a Registered National Historic
Landmark in 1971.

How the Government Works

Residents of Connecticut have always taken a strong interest in their government. The Fundamental Orders of 1639 said that the people had the right to choose their leaders and the right to limit their power. While England chose governors for most of its colonies, Connecticut's people elected their own governor.

Today, Connecticut has 169 towns. Each likes to be as independent as possible. People participate in town meetings and decide how a town should spend its money and run its affairs. This is called home rule. Local control and the power of each person's vote are still important in Connecticut.

Voters in each Connecticut town elect people to represent them. These representatives sometimes go by different names, depending on the town's type of government. Some small towns call each of their representatives a "selectman" who serve on the board of selectmen. The board conducts meetings throughout the year to discuss and vote on important issues that affect residents.

Larger towns and cities call their representatives "council members." They form a town or city council. Sometimes these towns also have a manager hired by the council to help run the town.

In some cities, voters elect a mayor. A mayor's power can vary. Depending on the city, the mayor can run the town or serve as a contact between the community and the local city board or council.

Connecticut has eight counties: Hartford, New Haven, Fairfield, Middlesex, Litchfield, Windham, Tolland, and New London. Counties are groups of towns and cities located near one another. Unlike most states, Connecticut does not have county governments. Towns and cities like their independence, so they often do not place great importance on working together to create and support legislation that goes beyond their local area.

Three State Branches

Connecticut's state government's structure is similar to the U.S. government's. It has three parts, or branches. The three branches coexist so that one branch does not have too much power.

Opening day ceremonies at the state capitol include swearing in ceremonies for new members of the Connecticut General Assembly.

Executive

The executive branch includes the governor, lieutenant governor, secretary of state, treasurer, comptroller, and attorney general. The governor either approves or vetoes (rejects) laws passed by the legislature. Approved laws are enforced by the governor and other executive agencies. The governor also appoints state officials and manages the state budget, which determines where the state spends its money. Governors are elected for four-year terms.

Legislative

The state house of representatives and the state senate form the Connecticut General Assembly, the state's legislative branch. Legislators propose and vote on laws for the state. There are thirty-six state senators and 151 state representatives. Senators represent larger areas than representatives, who focus more on smaller, local areas. All are elected for two-year terms.

The supreme court was created in 1818 when Connecticut adopted its constitution.

Judicial

The judicial branch includes a system of courts that make legal decisions on many levels. They decide whether people accused of crimes have actually broken a law. They rule on disputes between individuals or companies. In addition, the courts can decide if state laws are legal under the Connecticut constitution. The judicial system includes superior courts that handle most criminal trials and lawsuits brought by one citizen against another. If someone loses a court decision they can appeal (ask for the decision to be changed), first to appellate courts and then to the Supreme Court of Connecticut.

United States Senators and Congressmen

Like other states, Connecticut voters choose people to represent them in the U.S. Congress in Washington, D.C. Voters in five Connecticut regions, called districts, elect one House member for a two-year term. Voters from across the state elect two U.S. senators for a six-year term.

How a Bill Becomes a Law

State legislators propose laws (called bills until they are passed) to address state issues. Sometimes the ideas behind a bill come from the state's residents.

State police detective Barbara J. Mattson displays the gun model used in the Sandy Hook School shooting during a subcommittee hearing.

A senator or representative must introduce the bill in his or her own house. Then, a committee in that house will discuss and perhaps alter the bill. If the committee approves the bill, it goes to all the members of the same house. If members vote to approve it, the bill moves to the other house.

Members in the second house then discuss the bill. If they also agree, it goes to the governor to be approved. If the second house decides to revise the bill and then approves it, the revised version may go back to the first house for another vote.

In some cases, members from both houses get together to merge different versions of the same bill passed by each house. Then both houses must vote to approve the new common version.

When a bill passed by both houses gets to the governor, he or she can accept or reject it. When the governor accepts it, it becomes law. If the governor vetoes the bill, it can still become a law if two-thirds of the members in each house vote to override the veto. Sometimes a bill can become law if the governor takes no action and neither accepts nor rejects it.

The aftermath of the tragic shooting in Sandy Hook, Connecticut demonstrates the way that laws are passed in the State.

On December 14, 2012, twenty-six people—twenty students and six adults—were shot and killed at the Sandy Hook Elementary School in Newtown, Connecticut, by Adam Lanza, 20, who first shot and killed his mother in their home.

The Connecticut legislature reacted quickly. First, a task force of legislators set out to determine ways to prevent future mass school shootings. They decided that a change to Connecticut's gun laws would help. After long legislative sessions that sometimes lasted well into the night, the state's house of representatives and senate both passed bipartisan gun control legislation. Bipartisan means that the bill had the support of both the Democratic and the Republican parties.

Following the votes, the senate and house merged their different bills into one final version, which was then signed by Connecticut Governor Dannel Malloy. The law completed a three-month process that began shortly after the December 14 massacre.

POLITICAL FIGURES
FROM CONNECTICUT

Christopher Dodd:
United States Senator, 1981-2011

Chris Dodd, of Willimantic, Connecticut, served as a Peace
Corps volunteer in the Dominican Republic in the 1960s.
He co-authored the Dodd-Frank Wall Street Reform and
Protection Act, with representative Barney Frank.
It was written to prevent the 2008 financial crisis
from happening again.

Dannel Patrick Malloy:
Governor of Connecticut, 2011-

The Stamford native struggled to overcome learning and
physical disabilities, eventually gaining the skills he needed
to attend Boston College and Boston College Law School.
He served as Stamford's mayor for 14 years before being
elected governor in November 2010.

Jodi Rell:
Governor of Connecticut, 2004-2011

She became the ninth woman governor in United States
history and the second in Connecticut when she replaced
John Rowland, who faced corruption charges, on July 1, 2004.
A breast cancer survivor, she was credited with stabilizing
the state after replacing Rowland.

CONNECTICUT

YOU CAN MAKE A DIFFERENCE

Contacting Lawmakers

One way people get involved in politics is by contacting members of the legislature, either to give elected officials their views or to get information about what elected officials are doing.

You can find a list of state representatives at:
www.cga.ct.gov/asp/menu/hlist.asp

State senators can be found at:
www.cga.ct.gov/asp/menu/slist.asp

Start Local

In Connecticut, with so many decisions made in the towns, one way to take action is to write your selectman. Each town has a website with contact information. Selectmen vote on local issues, and can make their communities leaders in the region on matters you favor.

A town meeting in Weston called to discuss high school renovations in 2013.

This happened when some lawmakers and citizens took steps to make Connecticut a greener state. In September 2008, Westport's legislative body passed a bill banning the use of plastic shopping bags. Under the rule, a store that distributes plastic bags can be fined $150. The ban went into effect on March 19, 2009.

Westport is known for being progressive, so it was not a surprise to see the measure pass by a vote of 25 to 6. A state representative from the Westport area introduced a bill to ban plastic bags in Connecticut, but it was rejected. In January 2014, a proposal to discourage the use of plastic bags by charging a fee for them was introduced.

To contact your national leaders, visit www.cga.ct.gov/asp/menu/cgafindleg.asp and type in your address. A list of your legislators will be displayed. Find links to your representatives and senator, and use the email links to express your concerns.

Stamford is growing, combining the old with the new.

Making a Living

Connecticut's workers have jobs that are both old and new. Farmers still raise crops and animals like the Native Americans and first settlers did. Factory workers still turn out equipment, following the example of early Connecticut craftspeople. However, Connecticut is also building cutting-edge industries based on new technology. Many of Connecticut's new businesses focus on the growing medical, media, and entertainment industries.

While agriculture no longer holds its once-prominent position in Connecticut's economy, farming is still important. Connecticut farmers produce nearly $600 million worth of agricultural products each year. However, sometimes it costs too much to run a farm. An easier way for farmers to make money is to sell their farms to corporations that would like to develop—or build on—their land. Connecticut loses some farmland each year to development. A state program called the Farmland Preservation Program gives farmers money so they can keep working their land instead of selling it to developers who build houses, stores, or offices. Through 2013 the program has protected 297 farms totaling almost 38,000 acres.

10 KEY INDUSTRIES

Aerospace Technology

Agriculture

Casinos

1. Aerospace Technology

Aerospace technology includes the manufacturing of aircraft and other equipment. Connecticut is a leading producer of aerospace products. Sikorsky helicopters and Pratt & Whitney aircraft engines are designed and made in Connecticut.

2. Agriculture and Aquaculture

Connecticut's most important crops are dairy, poultry, nursery plants, tobacco, vegetables, and fruit. Connecticut also has a large **aquaculture** industry. This means raising fish and other water animals for food. Many varieties of fish, as well as oysters, lobsters, and other shellfish, are caught in Long Island Sound.

3. Casinos

A large part of the state's growth in tourism can be credited to the two casinos and resorts operated by Native American tribes. The two casinos, as well as the resorts' hotels, restaurants, and other facilities, provide many jobs in the southeastern part of the state.

4. Health Care

Health care and health insurance continue to become more and more important in the United States and in Connecticut. Health care and social assistance companies employ more than 270,000 workers in the state.

5. Insurance

Companies offering all kinds of insurance play a major role in Connecticut's economy. Hartford, long known as the "Insurance Capital of the World," is home to many large insurance companies including Aetna and The Hartford Financial Services Group.

6. Media and Entertainment

Media companies continue to increase their presence in Connecticut. ESPN employs more than four thousand people at its headquarters and studios in Bristol. The Yankees Entertainment and Sports (YES) Network, the NBC Sports Group, the NHL Network, and World Wrestling Entertainment (WWE) are in Stamford.

7. Medical Research

In laboratories across the state, Connecticut scientists look for medicines that can cure or prevent sickness. The state's universities also contribute to the medical research needed to help people.

8. Seafood

The seafood industry is very important to Connecticut. Millions of pounds of seafood are harvested every year, bringing more than $100 million to the state's economy. Oysters, shrimp, and shad are just some examples of Connecticut seafood. The state's seafood festivals and restaurants also bring in money.

9. Submarines

Connecticut has a long history of making the world's best submarines. The U.S. Navy recently renewed its funding with a company named Electric Boat in Groton to continue to build submarines.

10. Tourism

Tourism is a major source of jobs in Connecticut, where people come to experience beautiful fall foliage, live entertainment, and marine life.

Media and Entertainment

Medical Research

Submarines

Manufacturing

Connecticut has lost many manufacturing jobs in recent years. Some companies moved out of state. Others that used to work for the U.S. military received fewer orders to make goods, so the companies had to lay off workers.

However, manufacturers in Connecticut still make many things and about one out of every nine residents still work in this field. The state's largest manufacturing companies build advanced products like aircraft engines, helicopters, and submarines for aircraft companies and the United States military. Other companies are involved in metalworking, electronics, and plastics. Producing all these things requires skilled workers. Connecticut is known for its well-trained machinists and engineers.

Connecticut is also the home to many interesting—and fun—products. Connecticut is the birthplace of the Wiffle ball. The plastic bats and balls are still made in the state. Another Connecticut product is PEZ. Since 1972, all the PEZ candy eaten in the United States has been produced in a factory in Orange, Connecticut. This is good for the state's economy since PEZ is now sold in more than eighty countries around the world!

All PEZ candy in the United States is made in Connecticut.

Making Modern Technology

Connecticut's long history as a place for new technologies and inventions continues today. The state is a leader in the field of biotechnology, often referred to in its shortened form "biotech." Scientists are studying genes, which are tiny chemicals found in every living thing. Genes control how a plant or animal looks and how it survives. Scientists can use different genes to create new drugs, treat some illnesses, or make plants that grow faster. Connecticut is becoming a center for biotechnology research and has a specialized job concentration in two of the bioscience subsectors—drugs and pharmaceuticals. The state is also highly concentrated in a third subsector: research, testing, and medical laboratories.

Connecticut companies of all sizes also use science and computers to create more advanced products. Small computer software businesses have been coming to the state. Other state companies are involved with the Internet and making computer parts.

One teenage Connecticut inventor turned to science to create an important new product that has improved people's health. In 2001, Michael Nyberg of Old Lyme found that certain high sounds can kill mosquitoes before they become adults. The adult mosquitoes bite people and sometimes carry deadly diseases, such as West Nile virus. "I knew I wanted to do a project in acoustics [sound]," Nyberg said. "We had this big

Herb Nyberg demonstrates the Larvasonic, which was made by his son to kill dangerous mosquitoes.

Recipe for Joe Froggers Cookies

Molasses-spice cookies date back to the colonial era. According to legend, this version is named after Joseph Brown, a free African American man who served in the Revolutionary War and opened a tavern next to a frog pond. When the batter was added to the skillet, it formed shapes that looked like frogs. This recipe uses two popular Connecticut ingredients: molasses and nutmeg.

What You Need

1/2 cup (118 milliliters) shortening

1 cup (236.5 mL) white sugar

1 cup (236.5 mL) dark molasses

1/2 (118 mL) cup water

4 cups (946 mL) all-purpose flour

1 1/2 teaspoons (7.3 mL) salt

1 teaspoon (5 mL) baking soda

1 1/2 teaspoons (7.3 mL) ground ginger

1/2 teaspoon (2.5 mL) ground cloves

1/2 teaspoon (2.5 mL) ground nutmeg

1/4 teaspoon (1.2 mL) ground allspice

What to Do

1. In a large bowl, cream shortening and sugar together. Mix in molasses and water. Sift together flour, salt, baking soda, ginger, cloves, nutmeg, and allspice in a bowl; blend into the shortening mixture. Cover and chill overnight.

2. Preheat oven to 375°F (190°C). Lightly grease cookie sheets. Roll out cookie dough 1/4 inch thick on floured surface. Cut with 3-inch cookie cutter and arrange on prepared cookie sheets. Sprinkle cookies with additional sugar (optional).

3. Bake until cookies are set up and very lightly browned, 10 to 12 minutes. You need to leave cookies on cookie sheet for 2 minutes after baking to keep them from breaking.

West Nile scare, and I . . . kind of put the two together." For a science project, Nyberg built a device, now called the Larvasonic, to test his idea about using sound to kill the mosquitoes. The machine worked! Now, Michael and his family run a company to sell the machines. Forty machines have been sold to government agencies since they went on sale in 2012. They cost $4,500 each.

A Good Kind of FIRE

More than 160,000 Nutmeggers work in a group of industries sometimes called FIRE: finance, insurance, and real estate. In Connecticut, insurance and finance stand out as the largest companies.

The state's first insurance company opened in Hartford in 1810. Hartford continues as an important insurance center today. Stamford has grown as a financial and media center, in part because it is so close to New York City with easy access by car and train. Many financial companies based in New York have offices in the Stamford area, and some companies have even moved their headquarters from New York City to Stamford.

Companies involved in FIRE are sometimes called service industries. Other

Stamford's transportation system has helped it attract business.

The Travelers Tower at the far left is a familiar site on the Hartford skyline.

service jobs include selling goods in stores, providing legal services and medical care, and working for schools. More than 800,000 Nutmeggers work in all these other service industries.

Government is also a big employer in Connecticut. Nearly sixty-five thousand people work for the government at the local, state, and national levels.

Tourism

Tourism is one part of the service industry that has grown in Connecticut. People from around the country—and around the world—like to visit Connecticut for several reasons. In the fall, many visitors come to parts of the state to admire the beautiful scenery and the colorful foliage. People visit the state during other parts of the year, looking to relax in the peace and quiet of Connecticut's countryside, participate in winter sports or take a summer swim. They might also want to visit historic spots, such as the Mystic Seaport restored whaling village and Connecticut Freedom Trail sites honoring the state's African American heritage.

The state's cities also have a lot to offer tourists, including museums and fine restaurants. Many Nutmeggers work in the theaters, museums, and stores that tourists often visit. Whatever their reasons, and whichever part of the state tourists visit, they will need to stay and eat at Connecticut's hotels and restaurants. Not only do these businesses bring money into the state, but they also provide jobs for many Nutmeggers.

What Does the Future Hold?

The economy across the United States began to suffer in 2008 and the downturn lasted until 2010. As the country entered a severe recession, workers in Connecticut felt the effects and more than 119,000 Nutmeggers lost their jobs. Between 2010 and 2013, Connecticut recovered about half of the jobs that were lost, but growth remains slow.

Among all U.S. states, Connecticut still has one of the highest percentages of residents who are college graduates. These educated workers will continue to make useful new products and start new companies. Yankee ingenuity is still strong in Connecticut. Nutmeggers from all walks of life and all different fields will work together to help their state continue to grow and move into the future.

The Mystic Seaport's Museum of America and the Sea provides opportunities for hands-on learning.

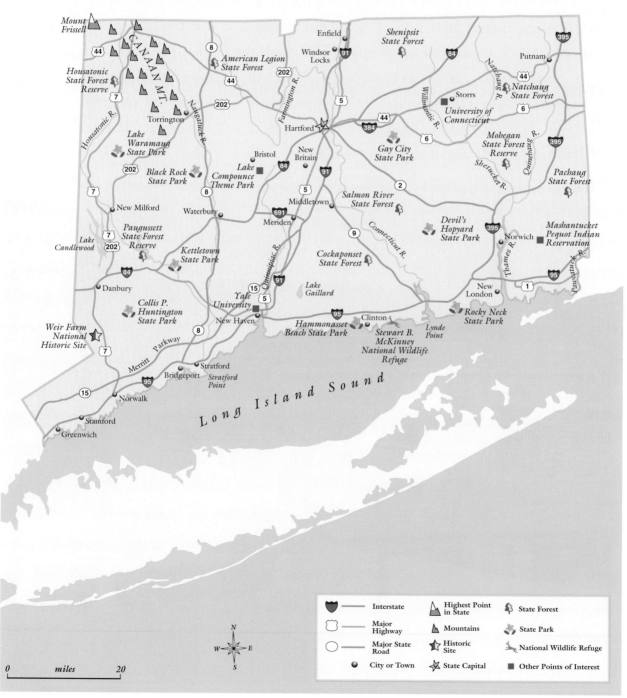

Mount Frissell

CANAAN MT.

44

8

Enfield

Shenipsit State Forest

84

395

Putnam

American Legion State Forest

Windsor Locks

91

44

Natchaug State Forest

Housatonic State Forest Reserve

7

44

202

202

Hartford

5

Storrs

University of Connecticut

6

44

Mohegan State Forest Reserve

6

395

Torrington

Naugatuck R.

Farmington R.

384

Willimantic R.

Natchaug R.

Quinebaug R.

Shetucket R.

Pachaug State Forest

Lake Waramaug State Park

Bristol

New Britain

Gay City State Park

Housatonic R.

202

Black Rock State Park

84

91

2

7

Lake Compounce Theme Park

8

5

Middletown

Salmon River State Forest

Devil's Hopyard State Park

395

Norwich

Mashantucket Pequot Indian Reservation

New Milford

Waterbury

691

Meriden

9

Connecticut R.

Thames R.

7

Paugussett State Forest Reserve

202

Kettletown State Park

Cockaponset State Forest

New London

1

95

Lake Candlewood

7

Quinnipiac R.

Pawcatuck R.

84

Danbury

Collis P. Huntington State Park

15

91

Lake Gaillard

95

Clinton

Rocky Neck State Park

Weir Farm National Historic Site

8

5

Yale University

New Haven

Hammonasset Beach State Park

Stewart B. McKinney National Wildlife Refuge

Lynde Point

7

Merritt Parkway

Stratford

Bridgeport

Stratford Point

15

Norwalk

95

Stamford

Greenwich

Long Island Sound

Legend

Interstate	Highest Point in State
Major Highway	Mountains
Major State Road	Historic Site
City or Town	State Capital
State Forest	
State Park	
National Wildlife Refuge	
Other Points of Interest	

N
W E
S

0   miles   20

CONNECTICUT
MAP SKILLS

1. What is the highest point in Connecticut?

2. Yale University is located close to what city?

3. How many different interstate highways are in Connecticut?

4. What Connecticut town or city is furthest north on the map?

5. Lake Candlewood is between what two Connecticut cities/towns?

6. What university is located close to Storrs, Connecticut?

7. If you started at Stamford and drove northeast on Interstate 95, what is the next town or city you would drive through?

8. The Mashantucket Pequot Reservation is located in what corner of the state (northeast, northwest, southeast, or southwest)?

9. Hammonasset Beach State Park is on what body of water?

10. What mountains can be found between the Hausatonic River and the Naugatuck River?

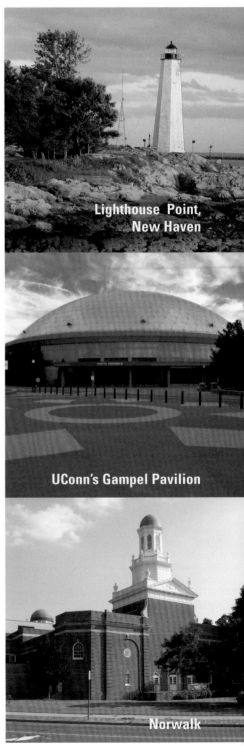

Lighthouse Point, New Haven

UConn's Gampel Pavilion

Norwalk

10. Canaan Mountains
9. Long Island Sound
8. Southeast
7. Norwalk
6. University of Connecticut (UConn)
5. Danbury and New Milford
4. Enfield
3. 6 (Interstates 84, 91, 95, 384, 395, 691)
2. New Haven
1. Mount Frissell

State Flag, Seal, and Song

Connecticut's flag shows the state coat of arms on a blue background. The streamer below the shield has the state motto in Latin. *Qui Transtulit Sustinet* means "He Who Transplanted Still Sustains."

The state seal bears the same symbols as the coat of arms. It is believed that the three grapevines represent early colonial settlements in the area. The Latin translation for "Seal of the State of Connecticut" is printed around the seal. This version of the seal was adopted in 1931.

Connecticut adopted its official state song, "Yankee Doodle," in 1978. The song was originally sung by British soldiers to mock American fighters during the Revolutionary War, but the Americans proudly took it for their own when they started winning battles.

Visit the following link to see the lyrics and hear "Yankee Doodle":

www.ct.gov/ctportal/cwp/view.asp?a=885&q=246520

Glossary

Amistad The name of a slave transport ship a group of African slaves revolted against their captors in 1839. The ship arrived in New London and the Africans eventually won their freedom in court.

Appalachian Trail The longest marked footpath in the United States. Almost 2,200 miles (3,540 km) long, it passes through fourteen states, including western Connecticut.

aquaculture The business of raising fish and other water animals for food.

endangered Living things like animals, plants, or fish whose numbers are so small that they are at risk of disappearing completely.

ethnicity A group of people who share cultural characteristics such as nationality, culture, ancestry, language, and beliefs.

hydroelectricity Generating electric power by converting the energy of running or falling water (such as rivers or waterfalls) into electricity.

immigrants People who leave one country and come to another to live there.

Ivy League A group of eight colleges and universities in the northeastern U.S., including Yale University in Connecticut, with a reputation for high scholastic and social prestige.

legislature An organization of people with the power to make or change laws. They are usually elected by the people they represent.

nor'easters Severe storms that often form off the East Coast in the Atlantic Ocean and then move up the east coast into New England and Canada. A nor'easter gets its name from its strong winds from the northeast. These storms often include heavy winds, snow, rain, and waves that crash onto coastal areas.

nutmeg Spice from the seed produced by a nutmeg tree. Nutmeg is often used in pies, puddings, cakes, and cookies. Due to its popularity, Connecticut is often nicknamed the Nutmeg State, and its people are called Nutmeggers.

peddlers People who travels from place to place selling small goods in small amounts.

prosperous Financial success, and having a lot of material goods.

Puritans A group of people who left England to escape persecution and to practice their religion in new lands. Most found their way to New England.

sandbars Ridges of sand in bodies of water formed by waves and currents, making it difficult for boats to pass.

whaling The hunting of whales for food and oil.

More About Connecticut

BOOKS

Burgan, Michael. *Voices from Colonial America: Connecticut 1614–1776*. Washington, DC: National Geographic Children's Books, 2007.

Cantele, Andi Marie. *Explorers Guide Connecticut (Eighth Edition)*. Woodstock, VT: The Countryman Press, 2012

Faude, Wilson H. *Hidden History of Connecticut*. Charleston, SC: The History Press, 2010.

Lavin, Lucianne. *Connecticut's Indigenous Peoples*. New Haven, CT: Yale University Press, 2012

WEBSITES

ConneCT Kids—The Official State of Connecticut Website for Children:
www.kids.ct.gov/kids/site/default.asp

CT.gov: The Official Web Site for the State of Connecticut:
www.ct.gov

CTvisit.com: The Connecticut Office of Tourism's Website:
www.ctvisit.com/connections/family-fun

ABOUT THE AUTHORS

Michael Burgan has written more than 150 fiction and nonfiction books for children, and is a recipient of an Educational Press Association of America award.

Stephanie Fitzgerald is the author of more than twenty books and lives in Stamford, Connecticut, with her husband and their daughter.

Gerry Boehme is an author, speaker, and business consultant from New York City. He has published many articles dealing with media and trends.

Index

Page numbers in **boldface** are illustrations.

Index